D0783821

THE BLOOMSBURY BOOK OF

Christmas Poems

For John Mole with
love and gratitude

THE BLOOMSBURY BOOK OF

Christmas Poems

ILLUSTRATED BY TOM SAECKER

BLOOMSBURY

First published in Great Britain in 1998
Bloomsbury Publishing Plc, 38 Soho Square, London, W1V 5DF

Copyright © Text This Selection Fiona Waters 1998
Copyright © Illustrations Tom Saecker 1998

The moral right of the author has been asserted
A CIP catalogue record of this book is available from the
British Library

ISBN 0 7475 4028 4

Printed in England

10 9 8 7 6 5 4 3 2 1

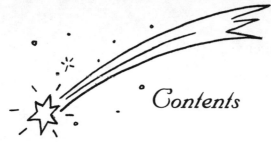

Contents

The Shepherds' Carol

We stood on the hills, Lady,
Our day's work done,
Watching the frosted meadows
That winter had won.

The evening was calm, Lady,
The air so still,
Silence more lovely than music
Folded the hill.

There was a star, Lady,
Shone in the night,
Larger than Venus it was
And bright, so bright.

Oh, a voice from the sky, Lady,
It seemed to us then
Telling of God being born
In the world of men.

And so we have come, Lady,
Our day's work done,
Our love, our hopes, ourselves
We give to your son.

Anonymous

Winds Through the Olive Trees

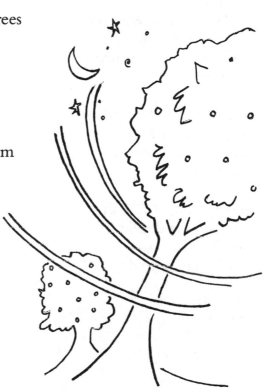

Winds through the olive trees
softly did blow,
round little Bethlehem
long, long ago.

Sheep on the hillsides lay,
white as the snow;
shepherds were watching them
long, long ago.

Then from the happy skies
angels bent low
singing their songs of joy
long, long ago:

For, in his manger bed
cradled, we know,
Christ came to Bethlehem
long, long ago.

French Traditional

Carol of the Brown King

Of the three Wise Men
Who came to the King,
One was a brown man,
So they sing.

Of the three Wise Men
Who followed the Star,
One was a brown king
From afar.

They brought fine gifts
Of spices and gold
In jewelled boxes
Of beauty untold.

Unto His humble
Manger they came
And bowed their heads
In Jesus' name.

Three Wise Men,
One dark like me –
Part of His
Nativity.

Langston Hughes

King Herod and the Cock

There was a star in David's land,
　　So bright it did appear
Into King Herod's chamber,
　　And brightly it shined there.

The Wise Men soon espied it,
　　And told the king on high,
A princely babe was born that night
　　No king could e'er destroy.

'If this be true,' King Herod said,
    'As thou hast told to me,
This roasted cock that lies in the dish
    Shall crow full fences three.'

The cock soon thrustened and feathered well,
    By the work of God's own hand,
And he did crow full fences three,
    In the dish where he did stand.

                    Traditional

El Noi de la Mare
THE SON OF THE VIRGIN

What shall we give to the Son of the Virgin?
What can we give Him that He will enjoy?
First, we shall give Him a tray full of raisins,
Then we shall offer sweet figs to the Boy.

What shall we give the beloved of Mary?
What can we give to her beautiful Child?
Raisins and olives and figs and sweet honey,
Candy and figs and a cheese that is mild.

What shall we do if the figs are not ripened?
What shall we do if the figs are still green?
If by Palm Sunday they still have not ripened,
Yet shall that ripeness at Easter be seen.

Catalan Traditional

Torches

Torches, torches, run with torches
All the way to Bethlehem!
Christ is born and now lies sleeping;
Come and sing your song to him!

Ah, Ro-ro, Ro-ro, my baby,
Ah, Ro-ro, my love, Ro-ro;
Sleep you well, my heart's own darling,
While we sing you our Ro-ro.

Sing, my friends, and make you merry,
Joy and mirth and joy again;
Lo, he lives, the King of heaven,
Now and evermore, Amen.

Galacian Traditional

Mice in the hay

Out of the lamplight
    whispering worshipping
the mice in the hay

timid eyes pearl-bright
    whispering worshipping
whisking quick and away

they were there that night
    whispering worshipping
smaller than snowflakes are

quietly made their way
    whispering worshipping
close to the manger

yes, they were afraid
    whispering worshipping
as the journey was made

from a dark corner
  whispering worshipping
scuttling together

but He smiled to see them
  whispering worshipping
there in the lamplight

stretched out His hand to them
  they saw the baby King
hurried back out of sight
  whispering worshipping

                Leslie Norris

Shepherds' Carol

Three practical farmers from back of the dale –
    Under the high sky –
On a Saturday night said 'So long' to their sheep
That were bottom of dyke and fast asleep –
    When the stars came out in the Christmas sky.

They called at the pub for a gill of ale –
    Under the high sky –
And they found in the stable, stacked with the corn,
The latest arrival, newly-born –
    When the stars came out in the Christmas sky.

They forgot their drink, they rubbed their eyes –
    Under the high sky –
They were tough as leather and ripe as a cheese
But they dropped like a ten-year-old down on their knees –
    When the stars came out in the Christmas sky.

They ran out in the yard to swap their news –
　　Under the high sky –
They pulled off their caps and roused a cheer
To greet a spring lamb before New Year –
　　When the stars came out in the Christmas sky.

Norman Nicholson

Talking Turkeys!!

Be nice to yu turkeys dis christmas
Cos turkeys jus wanna hav fun
Turkeys are cool, turkeys are wicked
An every turkey has a Mum.
Be nice to yu turkeys dis christmas,
Don't eat it, keep it alive,
It could be yu mate an not on yu plate
Say, Yo! Turkey I'm on your side.

I got lots of friends who are turkeys
An all of dem fear christmas time,
Dey wanna enjoy it, dey say humans destroyed it
An humans are out of dere mind,
Yeah, I got lots of friends who are turkeys
Dey all hav a right to a life,
Not to be caged up an genetically made up
By any farmer an his wife.

Turkeys jus wanna play reggae
Turkeys jus wanna hip-hop
Can you imagine a nice young turkey saying,

'I cannot wait for de chop?'
Turkeys like getting presents, dey wanna watch christmas TV,
Turkeys hav brains an turkeys feel pain
In many ways like yu an me.

I once knew a turkey called Turkey
He said 'Benji explain to me please,
Who put de turkey in christmas
An what happens to christmas trees?'
I said, 'I am not too sure turkey
But it's nothing to do wid Christ Mass
Humans get greedy an waste more dan need be
An business men mek loadsa cash.'

Be nice to yu turkey dis christmas
Invite dem indoors fe sum greens
Let dem eat cake an let dem partake
In a plate of organic grown beans,
Be nice to yu turkey dis christmas
An spare dem de cut of de knife,
Join Turkeys United an dey'll be delighted
An yu will mek new friends '**FOR LIFE**'.

Benjamin Zephaniah

The Donkey's Christmas

Plodding on,
From inn to inn,
No room to spare,
No room but a stable bare.
We rest,
And the following morning Jesus is born.
I gaze on the wondrous sight.
The King is born,
The King in a stable.
I see great lights,
Lights that are angels.
Everyone comes to see this sight.
I carried Mary,
Holy Mary,
Last night.

Anonymous

Mary had a Baby

Mary had a baby, O Lord.
Mary had a baby, O my Lord.
Mary had a baby, O Lord.
The people keep a comin' and the train done gone.

Laid Him in a manger, O Lord.
Laid Him in a manger, O my Lord.
Laid Him in a manger, O Lord.
The people keep a comin' and the train done gone.

Shepherds came to see Him, O Lord.
Shepherds came to see Him, O my Lord.
Shepherds came to see Him, O Lord.
The people keep a comin' and the train done gone.

Named Him King Jesus, O Lord.
Named Him King Jesus, O my Lord.
Named Him King Jesus, O Lord.
The people keep a comin' and the train done gone.

Traditional Spiritual

In the Bleak Mid-Winter

In the bleak mid-winter
    Frosty wind made moan,
Earth stood hard as iron,
    Water like a stone;
Snow had fallen, snow on snow,
    Snow on snow,
In the bleak mid-winter
    Long ago.

Our God, Heaven cannot hold him
    Nor earth sustain;
Heaven and earth shall flee away
    When he comes to reign;
In the bleak mid-winter
    A stable-place sufficed
The Lord God Almighty
    Jesus Christ.

Enough for him, whom cherubim
　　Worship night and day,
A breastful of milk
　　And a mangerful of hay;
Enough for him, whom angels
　　Fall down before,
The ox and ass and camel
　　Which adore.

Angels and archangels
　　May have gathered there,
Cherubim and seraphim
　　Thronged the air;
But only his mother
　　In her maiden bliss
Worshipped the Beloved
　　With a kiss.

What can I give him,
    Poor as I am?
If I were a shepherd
    I would bring a lamb,
If I were a Wise Man
    I would do my part –
Yet what I can, I give him,
Give my heart.

Christina Rossetti

The Wicked Singers

And have you been out carol singing,
Collecting for the Old Folk's Dinner?

Oh yes indeed, oh yes indeed.

And did you sing all the Christmas numbers,
Every one a winner?

Oh yes indeed, oh yes indeed.

Good King Wenceslas, and Hark
The Herald Angels Sing?

Oh yes indeed, oh yes indeed.

And did you sing them loud and clear
And make the night sky ring?

Oh yes indeed, oh yes indeed.

And did you count up all the money?
Was it quite a lot?

Oh yes indeed, oh yes indeed.

And did you give it all to the Vicar,
Everything you'd got?

Certainly not, certainly not.

Kit Wright

Christmas is Coming

Christmas is coming
    The geese are getting fat,
Please to put a penny
    In the old man's hat.
If you haven't got a penny,
    A ha'penny will do;
If you haven't got a ha'penny,
    Then God bless you!

Traditional

Christmas Morn

Shall I tell you what will come
to Bethlehem on Christmas morn,
who will kneel them gently down
before the Lord new-born?

One small fish from the river,
with scales of red, red gold,
one wild bee from the heather,
one grey lamb from the fold,
one ox from the high pasture,
one black bull from the herd,
one goatling from the far hills,
one white, white bird.

And many children – God give them grace,
bringing tall candles to light Mary's face.

Ruth Sawyer

The Adoration of the Magi

It was the arrival of the kings
that caught us unawares;
we'd looked in on the woman in the barn,
curiosity you could call it,
something to do on a cold winter's night;
we'd wished her well –
that was the best we could do, she was in pain,
and the next thing we knew
she was lying on the straw
– the little there was of it –
and there was this baby in her arms.

It was, as I say, the kings
that caught us unawares . . .
Women have babies every other day,
not that we are there –
let's call it a common occurrence though,
giving birth. But kings
appearing in a stable with a
'Is this the place?' and kneeling,
each with his gift held out towards the child!

They didn't even notice us.
Their robes trailed on the floor,
rich, lined robes that money couldn't buy.
What must this child be
to bring kings from distant lands
with costly incense and gold?
What could a tiny baby make of that?

And what were we to make of
was it angels falling through the air,
entwined and falling as if from the rafters
to where the gaze of the kings met the child's
– assuming the child could see?
What would the mother do with the gift?
What would become of the child?
And we'll never admit there are angels

or that somewhere between
one man's eyes and another's
is a holy place, a space where a king could be
at one with a naked child,
at one with an astonished soldier.

Christopher Pilling

Wassailing Song

Wisselton, wasselton, who lives here?
We've come to taste your Christmas beer.
Up the kitchen and down the hall,
Holly, ivy, and mistletoe;
A peck of apples will serve us all,
Give us some apples and let us go.

Up with your stocking, on with your shoe,
If you haven't any apples, money will do.
My carol's done, and I must be gone,
No longer can I stay here.
God bless you all, great and small,
And send you a happy new year.

Traditional

Reindeer Report

Chimneys: colder.
Flightpaths: busier.
Driver: Christmas (F)
Still baffled by postcodes.

Children: more
And stay up later.
Presents: heavier.
Pay: frozen.

Mission in spite
Of all this
Accomplished.

U A Fanthorpe

Pilgrims in Mexico

'Who knocks at my door, so late in the night?'
'We are pilgrims, without shelter, and we want only a place to rest.'
'Go somewhere else and disturb me not again.'
'But the night is very cold. We have come from afar, and we are very
     tired.'
'But who are you? I know you not.'
'I am Joseph of Nazareth, a carpenter, and with me is Mary, my wife,
     who will be the mother of the Son of God.'
'Then come into my humble home, and welcome! And may the Lord
     give shelter to my soul when I leave this world!'

Traditional Mexican

I sing of a Maiden

I sing of a maiden
    That is makèless;
King of all kings
    To her son she ches.

He came all so still
    Where his mother was,
As dew in April
    That falleth on the grass.

He came all so still
    To his mother's bowr,
As dew in April
    That falleth on the flower.

He came all so still
    Where his mother lay,
As dew in April
    That falleth on the spray.

Mother and maiden
    Was never none but she;
Well may such a lady
    Godès mother be.

Traditional

How Far is it to Bethlehem?

How far is it to Bethlehem?
Not very far.
Shall we find a stable-room
Lit by a star?
Can we see the little child,
Is he within?
If we lift the wooden latch,
May we go in?

May we stroke the creatures there,
Ox, ass or sheep?
May we peep like them and see
Jesus asleep?
If we touch his tiny hand
Will he awake?
Will he know we've come so far
Just for his sake?

Great kings have precious gifts,
And we have naught.
Little smiles and little tears are
All we brought.
For all weary children
Mary must weep,
Here on his bed of straw,
Sleep, children, sleep.

Traditional

43

Christmas Day

There was a pig went out to dig
Christmas Day, Christmas Day,
There was a pig went out to dig.
On Christmas Day in the morning.

There was a cow went out to plough,
Christmas Day, Christmas Day,
There was a cow went out to plough,
On Christmas Day in the morning.

There was a sparrow went out to harrow,
Christmas Day, Christmas Day,
There was a sparrow went out to harrow,
On Christmas Day in the morning.

There was a drake went out to rake,
Christmas Day, Christmas Day,
There was a drake went out to rake,
On Christmas Day in the morning.

There was a crow went out to sow,
Christmas Day, Christmas Day,
There was a crow went out to sow,
On Christmas Day in the morning.

There was a sheep went out to reap,
Christmas Day, Christmas Day,
There was a sheep went out to reap,
On Christmas Day in the morning.

Traditional

Sans Day Carol

Now the holly bears a berry as white as the milk,
And Mary bore Jesus who was wrapped up in silk:

And Mary bore Jesus Christ our Saviour for to be,
And the first tree in the greenwood, it was the holly, holly, holly,
And the first tree in the greenwood, it was the holly.

Now the holly bears a berry as green as the grass,
And Mary bore Jesus who died on the cross:

Now the holly bears a berry as black as the coal,
And Mary bore Jesus who died for us all:

Now the holly bears a berry as blood is it red,
Then trust we our Saviour who rose from the dead:

Traditional Cornish

The Mayor and the Simpleton

They followed the Star to Bethlehem –
Boolo the baker, Barleycorn the farmer,
old Darby and Joan, a small boy Peter, and
a simpleton whose name was Innocent.
Over the snowfields and the frozen rutted lanes
they followed the Star to Bethlehem.

Innocent stood at the stable door
and watched them enter. A flower
stuck out of his yellow hair; his mouth gaped open
like a drawer that wouldn't shut.
He beamed upon the child where he lay
among the oxen, in swaddling clothes in the hay,
his blue eyes shining steady as the Star overhead;
beside him old Joseph and
Mary his mother, smiling.
                    Innocent was delighted.

They brought gifts with them – Boolo, some fresh crusty loaves
(warm from the baking) which he laid
at the feet of the infant Jesus, kneeling
in all humility.
     Innocent was delighted.

Barleycorn brought two baskets – one with a dozen eggs,
the other with two chickens – which he laid
at the feet of the infant Jesus, kneeling
in all humility.
     Innocent was delighted.

Darby and Joan brought apples and pears from their garden,
wrapped in her apron and stuffed
in the pockets of his trousers; the little boy
a pot of geraniums – he had grown them himself.
And they laid them
at the feet of the infant Jesus, kneeling
in all humility.
     Innocent was delighted.

The mayor rolled up in his coach with a jingle of bells
and a great to-do. He stepped out with a flourish
and fell flat on his face in the snow. His footmen
picked him up and opened his splended
crimson umbrella. Then he strutted to the door,
while the white flakes floated down
and covered it with spots. He was proud of his umbrella
and didn't mean to give it away.
Shaking the snow off on to the stable floor,
the mayor peered down at the child where he lay
among the oxen, in swaddling clothes in the hay,
his blue eyes shining steady as the Star overhead,
beside him old Joseph and
Mary his mother, smiling.

     Innocent was puzzled.

And the mayor said: 'On this important occasion
each must take a share in the general thanksgiving.
Hence the humble gifts – the very humble gifts –
which I see before me. My own contribution
is something special – a speech. I made it up myself and I'm sure
you'll all like it. Ahem. Pray silence for the mayor.'

'Moo, moo,' said the oxen.
'My fellow citizens,
the happy event I refer to – in which we all rejoice –
has caused a considerable stir
in the parish –'
    '– in the whole world,' said a voice.

Who spoke? Could it be Innocent, always so shy,
timid as a butterfly, frightened
as a sparrow with a broken wing? Yes, it was he.
Now God had made him bold.

    'I fear I must start again,' said the mayor.
'My fellow citizens, in the name of the people of this parish
I am proud to welcome one
who promises so well –'
    '– He is the Son of Heaven,'
said Innocent.

    The mayor took no notice.
'I prophesy a fine future for him,
almost – you might say – spectacular.
He'll do us all credit. At the same time I salute in particular
the child's mother, the poor woman who –'

'– She is not poor but the richest, most radiant
of mothers.'
    'Simpleton, how dare you interrupt!'
snapped the mayor.
But God, who loves the humble, heard him not.
He made him listen, giving Innocent the words:
'Mr Mayor, you don't understand. This birth
is no local event. The child is Jesus,
King of kings and Lord of lords.
A stable is his place and poverty his dwelling-place –
yet he has come to save the world. No speech
is worthy of him –'
    'Tush!' said the mayor.

'I took a lot of trouble. It's a rare
and precious gift, my speech – and now
I can't get a word in edgeways.'
    'Rare and precious, did you say? Hear what the child
has brought to *us* – peace on earth, goodwill toward men.
O truly rare and precious gift!'
    'Peace on earth,' said the neighbours,
'goodwill toward men. O truly rare
and precious gift!' They knelt in humility,
in gratitude to the child who lay

among the oxen, in swaddling clothes in the hay,
his blue eyes shining steady as the Star overhead,
beside him old Joseph and
Mary his mother, smiling.

The mayor was silent. God gave the simpleton
no more to say. Now
like a frightened bird
over the snowfields and the frozen rutted lanes
he fluttered away. Always, as before, a flower
stuck out of his yellow hair; his mouth gaped open
like a drawer that wouldn't shut.
He never spoke out like that again.

As for the mayor, he didn't finish his speech.
He called for his coach and drove off, frowning,
much troubled. For a little while
he thought of what the simpleton had said
But he soon forgot all about it, having
important business to attend to in town.

                                        Ian Serraillier

Country Carol

Walked on the crusted grass in the frosty air.
Blackbird saw me, gave me a gold-rimmed stare.

Walked in the winter woods where the snow lay deep.
Hedgehog heard me, smiled at me in his sleep.

Walked by the frozen pond where the ice shone pale.
Wind sang softly, moon dipped its silver sail.

Walked on the midnight hills till the star-filled dawn.
No one told me, I knew a king was born.

Sue Cowling

Carol of the Birds

From out of a wood a cuckoo did fly,
　　Cuckoo,
He came to a manger with joyful cry,
　　Cuckoo,
He hopped, he curtsied, round he flew,
And loud his jubilation grew,
　　Cuckoo, cuckoo, cuckoo.

A pigeon flew over to Galilee,
　　Vrercroo,
He strutted and cooed, and was full of glee,
　　Vrercroo,
And showed with jewelled wings unfurled,
His joy that Christ was in the world,
　　Vrercroo, vrercroo, vrercroo.

A dove settled down upon Nazareth,
    Tsucroo,
And tenderly chanted with all his breath,
    Tsucroo,
'Oh you,' he cooed, 'so good and true,
My beauty I do give to you,
    Tsucroo, tsucroo, tsucroo.'

Traditional

We Three Kings

We three kings of Orient are;
Bearing gifts we traverse afar,
Field and fountain, moor and mountain,
Following yonder star.

O star of wonder, star of night,
Star with royal beauty bright,
Westward leading, still proceeding,
Guide us to thy perfect light.

Melchior:

> Born a king on Bethlehem plain,
> Gold I bring, to crown him again,
> King forever, ceasing never,
> Over us all to reign.

Caspar:

Frankincense to offer have I,
Incense owns a deity nigh;
Prayer and praising, all men raising,
Worship him, God most high.

Balthazar:

Myrrh is mine; its bitter perfume
Breathes a life of gathering gloom;
Sorrowing, sighing, bleeding, dying,
Sealed in the stone-cold tomb.

All:

Glorious now behold him arise,
King and God and sacrifice,
Alleluia, alleluia,
Earth to the heav'ns replies.

John Henry Hopkins

Children of Frost

Children of frost
children of snow
a long way to go to Bethlehem.

        Children of dust
        children of sun
        the star told us to run to Bethlehem.

Out of the frost
out of the snow
we've brought a little fir tree to show to him.

        Out of the dust
        out of the sun
        we've brought a baby camel to bow low to him.

Holly sprigs
snow-laden twigs –

        baskets of figs in our arms –

a sheet of ice
edelweiss –

clusters of dates from our palms

cardamom and cloves
lemons from our groves –

sweet herbs to strew on his hay –

some coral beads
pomegranate seeds –

a rainbow we met on the way!

Mary, come,
show your son
to all the children of Bethlehem.
Hold him high,
let him see
all that our love can give to him.

Sue Cowling

Xmas

I forgot to send
A card to Jennie –
But the truth about cousins is
There's too many.

I also forgot
My Uncle Joe
But I believe I'll let
That old rascal go.

I done bought
Four boxes now
I can't afford
No more, no how.

So Merry Xmas,
Everybody!
Cards or no cards
Here's HOWDY!

Langston Hughes

Christmas at our House

The Christmases at our house
Aren't like the pictures I've seen
On calendars and Christmas cards
Where all is joy serene,
Where red-faced husbands kiss their wives
Beneath sprigs of mistletoe
And fat little angels sing carols
And it always seems to snow.
For a start my Dad starts moaning
Before he's even out of bed
And Elvis, my brother, starts screaming
When his Action Man loses his head.
And Ann won't touch her turkey
And Elvis starts calling her names
And Dad overdoes the brandy
And the pudding bursts into flames,
Auntie May starts singing long, sad hymns
And the mongrel is sick on the mat
While Uncle George gets merry
On just three glasses of sherry
And spills custard all over the cat.

After tea we play disorganized games
And Gran faints away in her chair
And the games always end in tears and sulks
Because Elvis will never play fair.
Sharron falls out with her boyfriend,
Tina stops talking to hers,
Then we have to call the fire brigade
When Tom's head gets stuck in the stairs.
I breath a sigh of relief when midnight arrives
And the relations all disappear
Because I know for certain that Christmas Day
Won't be round for another whole year.

Gareth Owen

Christmas Ornaments

The boxes break
At the corners,
Their sides
Sink weak;

They are tied up
Every year
With the same
Grey string;

But under the split
Lids, a fortune
Shines; globes
Of gold and sapphire,

Silver spires and
Bells, jewelled
Nightingales with
Pearly tails.

Valerie Worth

Christmas Spider

My fine web sparkles:
Indoor star in the roof's night
Over the baby.

Michael Harrison

The Little Cradle Rocks Tonight

The little cradle rocks tonight in glory,
    Rocks in glory, rocks in glory,
The little cradle rocks tonight in glory,
    Telling of the Son of God,
    Telling of the Son of God, oh glory!
    Telling of the Son of God, oh glory!
    Telling of the Son of God.

Oh Mary, won't you rock the cradle gently,
    Rock it gently, gently,
Mary, won't you rock the cradle gently,
    Singing of the Son of God.
    Child of God, Son of God, Child of God.

Now glory be to Jesus, God on high,
God on high, God on high,
Now glory be to Jesus, God on high,
Bringing us to peace on earth.
Amen.

Traditional Spiritual

Room at the Inn

*D*raughty, husband, that stable.
She looked . . . warm, though.
Almost at home.
And you know, husband, I swear
it's not one mite as dark in there
as you'd have thought.
And that child – so still, so quiet.
Perhaps they'll need more straw?
It won't get any warmer, early hours.
Maybe we should bring them in?
Husband, you're not listening!

There is our bed . . .
but then with breakfast early
and so many travellers . . .
Well, *they* won't go tomorrow, surely?
Husband, did you see . . . ?
Husband!

Oh well, old man, dream on!
Some day we've had,
and then those two arriving,
with every nook and cranny gone!

Funny how those moths
circled the old lantern,
husband. Almost like . . .
almost as if those three . . .
but no, it couldn't be!
And the light,
you should have seen the light!
Oh, it flickered, but
so bright, so bright,
and night so still.
Draughty it is, that stable,
husband.

Judith Nicholls

The Shepherd's Dog

But on the windy hill
Under that sudden star
A blaze of radiant light
Frightened my master.

He got up, left our sheep,
Tramped over the moor.
And I, following,
Came to this open door.

Sidled in, settled down,
Head on my paws,
Glad to be here, away
From the wind's sharpness.

Such warmth is in this shed,
Such comfort from this Child,
That I forget my hard life,
Ignore the harsh world,

And see on my master's face
The same joy I possess,
The knowledge of peace,
True happiness.

Leslie Norris

A Christmas Carol

The Christ-child lay on Mary's lap,
    His hair was like a light.
(O weary, weary were the world,
    But here is all alright.)

The Christ-child lay on Mary's breast,
    His hair was like a star.
(O stern and cunning are the kings,
    But here the true hearts are.)

The Christ-child lay on Mary's heart,
    His hair was like a fire.
(O weary, weary is the world,
    But here the world's desire.)

The Christ-child stood at Mary's knee.
    His hair was like a crown,
And all the flowers looked up at Him,
    And all the stars looked down.

G K Chesterton

St Joseph and God's Mother

St Joseph and God's Mother
    They kept good company,
And they rode out of Nazareth
    So early in the day.

They found no place to rest in,
    No place in all the town,
And there they made an arbour,
    Of reeds and grasses brown.

St Joseph went to look for fire,
    No fire there could he see,
And when he came to Mary,
    The Babe was on her knee,
As white as is the milk,
    As red as rose was He.

St Joseph looked upon Him:
    'O what is this fair thing?
This is no child of mine,
    This comes from heaven's King.'

By there came three shepherds
    To wish Him a good day,
The two upon their fiddles,
    The third his bells did play.

And there they played sweet music,
    All for to make Him mirth;
Three hours have not gone yet
    Since our Saviour's birth.

'Dance, Maiden Mary,
    Dance, Mother mild,
And if you will dance with me,
    The ass will hold the child.'

'I will not dance, Joseph,
        My husband so dear,
But if you will dance for joy,
        Dance, husband, here.'

Joseph then began to dance
        With all his might and main;
The mother smiled and said to him
        'Joseph is young again.'

'And if I rejoice, Mary,
        Well ought that to be;
Here is born to us to-night
        The King of glory.'

                Anonymous Spanish

The Barn

'*I* am tired of this barn!' said the colt.
'And every day it snows.
Outside there's no grass any more
And icicles grow on my nose.
I am tired of hearing the cows
Breathing and talking together.
I am sick of these clucking hens.
I *hate* stables and winter weather!'

'Hush, little colt,' said the mare.
'And a story I will tell
Of a barn like this one of ours
And the wonders that there befell.
It was weather much like this,
And the beasts stood as we stand now
In the warm good dark of the barn –
A horse and an ass and a cow.'

'And sheep?' asked the colt. 'Yes, sheep,
And a pig and a goat and a hen.
All of the beasts of the barnyard,

The usual servants of men.
And into their midst came a lady
And she was cold as death,
But the animals leaned above her
And made her warm with their breath.'

'There was her baby born
And laid to sleep in the hay,
While music flooded the rafters
And the barn was as light as day.
And angels and kings and shepherds
Came to worship the babe from afar,
But we looked at him first of all creatures
By the bright strange light of a star!'

Elizabeth Coatsworth

Pudding Charms

Our Christmas pudding was made in November,
All they put in it, I quite well remember:
Currants and raisins, and sugar and spice,
Orange peel, lemon peel – everything nice
Mixed up together, and put in a pan.
'When you've stirred it,' said Mother, 'as much as you can,
We'll cover it over, that nothing may spoil it.'
That night, when we children were all fast asleep,
A real fairy godmother came crip-a-creep!

She wore a red cloak, and a tall steeple hat
(Though nobody saw her but Tinker, the cat!)
And out of her pocket a thimble she drew,
A button of silver, a silver horse-shoe,
And, whisp'ring a charm, in the pudding pan popped them,
Then flew up the chimney directly she dropped them;
And even old Tinker pretended he slept
(With Tinker a secret is sure to be kept!),
So nobody knew, until Christmas came round,
And there, in the pudding, these treasures we found.

Charlotte Druitt Cole

The Christmas Tree

They chopped her down in some far wood
A week ago,
Shook from her dark green spikes her load
Of gathered snow.
And brought her home at last, to be
Our Christmas show.

A week she shone, sprinkled with lamps
And fairy frost;
Now, with her boughs all stripped, her lights
And spangles lost,
Out in the garden here, leaning
On a broken post,

She sighs gently ... Can it be
She longs to go
Back to that far-off wood, where green
And wild things grow?
Back to her dark green sisters, standing
In wind and snow?

John Walsh

Now Thrice Welcome Christmas

Now thrice welcome, Christmas,
  Which brings us good cheer,
Minc'd pies and plum porridge,
  Good ale and strong beer;
With pig, goose, and capon,
  The best that can be,
So well doth the weather
  And our stomachs agree.

Observe how the chimneys
  Do smoke all about,
The cooks are providing
  For dinner, no doubt;
For those on whose tables
  No victuals appear,
O may they keep Lent
  All the rest of the year!

With holly and ivy
    So green and so gay,
We deck up our houses
    As fresh as the day,
With bays and rosemary,
    And laurel complete;
And every one now
    Is a king in conceit.

Anonymous

The Boots of Father Christmas

We're the boots of Father Christmas
And you ought to
Give more thought to
The boots of Father Christmas
When you're merry
With your sherry,
For the boots of Father Christmas
Have a hard time
And a charred time
When the boots of Father Christmas
Land on raw coals –
Oh, our poor soles!

So the boots of Father Christmas
Ask you nicely,
But precisely:
Save the boots of Father Christmas
From our top hate –
A red hot grate,
Help the boots of Father Christmas:
When the sleigh's nigh,

Let the blaze die,
Then the boots of Father Christmas
Will be jolly
As your holly.

We're the boots of Father Christmas,
Please remember
Next December.

Richard Edwards

Carol

$\mathcal{D}$eep in the fading leaves of night
There lay the flower that darkness knows,
Till winter stripped and brought to light
The most incomparable Rose
That blows, that blows.

The flashing mirrors of the snow
Keep turning and returning still:
To see the lovely child below
And hold him is their only will;
Keep still, keep still.

And to let go his very cry
The clinging echoes are so slow
That still his wail they multiply
Though he lie singing now below,
So low, so low.

Even the doves forget to grieve
And gravely to his greeting fly
And the lone places that they leave
All follow and are standing by
On high, on high.

W R Rodgers

Kid Stuff

The wise guys
tell me
That Christmas
is Kid Stuff . . .
Maybe they've got
something there —
Two thousand years ago
three wise guys
chased a star
across a continent
to bring
frankincense and myrrh
to a Kid
born in a manger
with an idea in his head . . .
                    And as the bombs
                    crash
                    all over the world today
                    the real wise guys know
                    that we've all got to go
                    chasing stars

again
in the hope
that we can get back
some of that
Kid Stuff
born two thousand years ago.

Frank Horne

Christmas Song

The trees are all bare not a leaf to be seen
And the meadows their beauty have lost.
Now winter has come and 'tis cold for man and beast,
And the streams they are,
And the streams they are all fast bound down with frost.

'Twas down in the farmyard where the oxen feed on straw,
They send forth their breath like the steam.
Sweet Betsy the milkmaid now quickly she must go,
For flakes of ice she finds,
For flakes of ice she find a-floating on her cream.

'Tis now all the small birds to the barn-door fly for food
And gently they rest on the spray.
A-down the plantation the hares do search for food,
And lift their footsteps sure,
Lift their footsteps sure for fear they do betray.

Now Christmas is come and our song is almost done
For we soon shall have the turn of the year.
So fill up your glasses and let your health go round,
For I wish you all,
For I wish you all a joyful New Year.

Traditional

Ceremony Upon Candlemas Eve

Down with the rosemary, and so
Down with the bays and mistletoe;
Down with the holly, ivy, all
Wherewith ye dressed the Christmas hall;
That so the superstitious find
No one least branch there left behind;
For look, how many leaves there be
Neglected there, maids, trust to me,
So many goblins you shall see.

Robert Herrick

The Other Shepherd

*O*h let them be, he muttered,
Let them plan their journey,
Let that brilliant interrupting stranger
Beckon them to Bethlehem.
A little fling won't hurt them,
A change of air might suit them,
Get this twitch out of their system
But they'll soon be back.

So then he broke a loaf
and drained a goatskin, then,
The wine still wet upon his lips
And sparkling in his beard like stars,
He nodded off . . .

Tired men prefer
Sleep to a great wonder.

John Mole